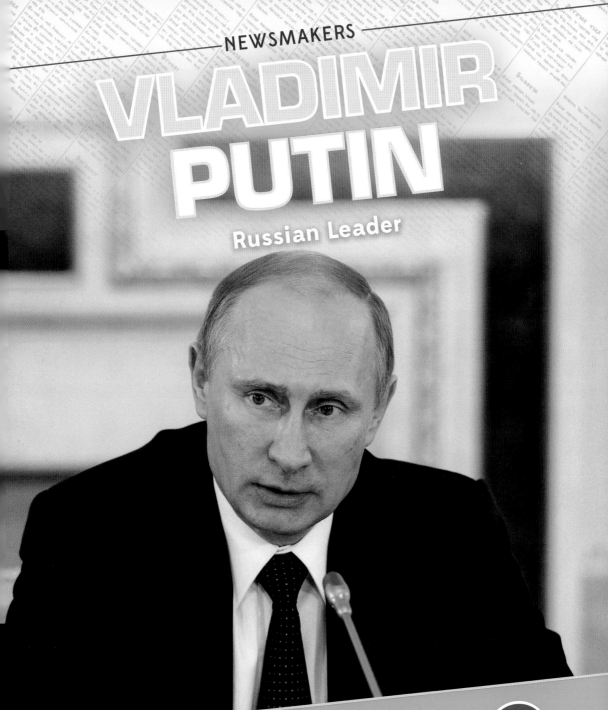

VLADIMIR
PUTIN

Russian Leader

by Lu Sylvan

Content Consultant
Daniel Mulholland
Professor
Tufts University

Core Library

An Imprint of Abdo Publishing
www.abdopublishing.com

www.abdopublishing.com

Published by Abdo Publishing, a division of ABDO, PO Box 398166, Minneapolis, Minnesota 55439. Copyright © 2015 by Abdo Consulting Group, Inc. International copyrights reserved in all countries. No part of this book may be reproduced in any form without written permission from the publisher. Core Library™ is a trademark and logo of Abdo Publishing.

Printed in the United States of America, North Mankato, Minnesota
092014
012015

Cover Photo: Mikhail Klimentyev/AP Images
Interior Photos: Mikhail Klimentyev/AP Images, 1, 32; AP Images, 4, 7, 10, 22; Red Line Editorial, 8, 39; iStockphoto, 12; epa/Corbis, 14; Alexei Druzhinin/AP Images, 17; Shutterstock Images, 20; Alexander Zemlianichenko/AP Images, 26, 30, 45; Ivan Sekretarev/AP Images, 29; RDM Studio/Shutterstock Images, 36; Frederic Legrand/Shutterstock Images, 38; Iurii Osadchi/Shutterstock Images, 40

Editor: Lauren Coss
Series Designer: Becky Daum

Library of Congress Control Number: 2014944237

Cataloging-in-Publication Data
Sylvan, Lu.
 Vladimir Putin: Russian leader / Lu Sylvan.
   p. cm. -- (Newsmakers)
Includes bibliographical references and index.
ISBN 978-1-62403-645-3
1. Putin, Vladimir Vladimirovich, 1952- --Juvenile literature. 2. Presidents--Russia (Federation)--Juvenile literature. 3. Russia (Federation)--Politics and government--1991- --Juvenile literature. 1.Title.
947.086/2092--dc23
[B]

2014944237

CONTENTS

CHAPTER ONE

A RELUCTANT PRESIDENT

The year 1999 was drawing to an end. Russian president Boris Yeltsin knew he was finished. The Russian economy had collapsed. Many officials and businessmen were accused of corruption. Yeltsin's opponents had already tried to force him out of office. Even his health was failing. Elections were coming up soon. With his approval rating so low, Yeltsin didn't think he could stay in power.

Although little information was known about Vladimir Putin when he became president of Russia in 1999, he would soon prove himself to be one of the world's most powerful leaders.

Conflicts between Russia and Chechnya have been frequent. When the Soviet Union collapsed in 1991, Chechnya declared itself an independent nation. Russia tried and failed to bring Chechnya back under full Russian control. The First Chechen War was fought from 1994 to 1996. Thousands of Russians and Chechens died in the conflict. Many of them were civilians. Russian forces left Chechnya after a peace treaty was signed in 1996. Then, in 1999, Islamist and separatist groups staged terrorist attacks on Russia. Putin accused Chechnya of being behind the attacks, leading to the brutal Second Chechen War. In 2003 Chechens voted to rejoin Russia. Some believe that the Russian government fixed the vote.

The Right Man for the Job?

Ten days before the new year began, Yeltsin called Russia's prime minister, Vladimir Putin, into his office. Putin was very popular with the Russian people. He seemed to be doing what the Russian people wanted. Putin had proven himself to be a firm and decisive leader. He had been very tough in battling terrorism. He was known for pushing for war in Chechnya, a small republic southwest of Russia. Though little was known about

Yeltsin, left, talks with Putin, right, shortly after Putin became president in December 1999.

his background, Putin seemed to be the perfect successor to Yeltsin.

Yeltsin told Putin that he was going to resign. As his second-in-command, Putin would automatically become acting president until the next election. Yeltsin wanted to know: Would Putin take the job or not?

Putin thought hard about it. Russia was the largest country in the world by area. The last few decades had brought many changes for the country. For most of the 1900s, Russia had been part of the

The Former Soviet Union

Look at the map showing what modern countries were created when the Soviet Union dissolved in 1991. Look at where rivers and major bodies of water are located. How does seeing this map help you better understand how the Soviet Union's breakup may have affected Russia's economy?

Soviet Union. This large country included many once-independent Asian and Eastern European countries. In 1991 the Soviet Union collapsed. Since then Russia had suffered from a poor economy, corruption, and frequent conflicts with the countries that had been part of the Soviet Union. Any president of Russia would have one of the most challenging jobs in the world.

Putin later said in an interview that it was not an easy decision. He wasn't sure he was ready. On the other hand, he knew it was a chance to serve Russia. He told Yeltsin yes.

On December 31, 1999, Yeltsin announced his resignation. Putin became Russia's acting president. He was officially elected to the presidency in March 2000.

A Controversial Leader

Putin would go on to be reelected president in 2004 and 2012. When he wasn't president, from 2008 to 2012, he

Putin's Family

Putin married flight attendant Lyudmila Shkrebneva in 1983. The couple had two daughters. Maria was born in 1985, and Ekaterina was born in 1986. Little is known about Putin's daughters. The Russian government has managed to protect the girls from the media. No confirmed photographs exist of the girls as adults. Putin and Lyudmila announced their divorce in 2013. Beyond that, little information is available about Putin's family.

served as Russia's prime minister. Throughout his time in office, Putin has been a controversial leader. He has been called a dictator. He has been accused of violating human rights. At times he has been a US ally. At other times, he has taken actions that are at odds with US leaders. Though Russia's relationships with other countries have been tense at times, Putin has kept firm control over what he believes are his country's best interests. In 2013 *Forbes* magazine named him the world's most powerful person.

Putin's actions affect people around the world. Conflicts continue to play out between Russia and its neighbors. The United States and other nations have objected to many of Putin's actions. Putin is frequently in the headlines.

EXPLORE ONLINE

Many world leaders are very careful about their public images. They try to create stories about themselves that may not always exactly match the truth. Read President Putin's official biography on the website below. Do you think he leaves out some things? Does he focus on some things to make himself seem like a certain kind of leader? Write your own biography, showing yourself in the best light. Think about which things you leave out.

Putin's Official Biography

www.mycorelibrary.com/vladimir-putin

CHAPTER TWO

A BOY WITH POTENTIAL

Vladimir Putin was born on October 7, 1952, in what was then called Leningrad, Russia. The city is now known as Saint Petersburg. His parents had lived through the Siege of Leningrad during World War II (1939–1945). At that time, German forces surrounded the city for more than 900 days. Few supplies were able to get into the city. More than 600,000 people died of disease

Vladimir grew up in Leningrad, Russia, which is now known as Saint Petersburg.

A school photo shows young Vladimir, front row and third from left.

and starvation. Two of Vladimir's brothers died there before he was born. But Vladimir's parents survived. His mother was 42 years old when he was born.

In and Out of Trouble

Vladimir started life in a family that was fairly poor. His father worked in a factory. His mother did odd jobs to help make ends meet. His family lived in a one-room apartment. Their food was usually cabbage soup and pancakes. For special occasions, his mother would make buns filled with rice, cabbage, and meat.

Vladimir's friends and teachers remember him as a troublemaker. He often got into fights. He caused so much trouble, he wasn't even allowed to join a club called the Pioneers. For a while, Vladimir was the only one in his class who wasn't in the group.

Discipline

When he was in sixth grade, though, everything changed. Like many boys, Vladimir thought about different jobs that he might do when he grew up. At one time, he wanted to be a sailor or a pilot. But he soon became fascinated by spy stories and movies about secret agents. Vladimir decided that he wanted to work for the KGB. The KGB was the security and intelligence agency for the Soviet Union. It accepted only the best candidates.

Vladimir began behaving well and getting good grades. Before long, he was even allowed into the Pioneers. Vladimir also started doing martial arts. He tried the Russian sport of sambo. Sambo is a little bit like wrestling. Eventually he switched to judo. Judo is a Japanese style of martial arts. It involves throws, holds, and chokes. Vladimir excelled at both sambo and judo. Judo helped Vladimir develop self-control skills. From then on, he became a better student. He focused on setting goals and achieving them.

A Bold Move

One day Vladimir marched up to the local office of the KGB. Though he was only in ninth grade, an official agreed to speak with him. Vladimir explained that he

wanted to get a job with the KGB. The official gave him an important piece of advice. A person can get into the KGB only after an army career, or if they complete higher education. The eager Vladimir asked what kind of higher education the official meant. The official said a law degree was best. Vladimir's school and career path were decided.

The young man may have had a clear direction for his future. But Vladimir's parents and coaches had different ideas. With his athletic skill, Vladimir was sure to get into the Academy of Civil Aviation. There he could be trained for a career as a pilot.

Competition to get into a university was much harder. If he weren't accepted, he would likely be forced to go into the army instead.

The KGB

KGB stands for *Komitet Gosudarstvennoy Bezopasnosti*. In English, that means Committee for State Security. It existed from 1954 to 1991. It was considered to be the world's most effective spy agency. It gathered information inside the Soviet Union. KGB members also spied in foreign countries. Many people feared the KGB. Young Vladimir was considered brave to walk into the spy office and ask questions. The KGB was known to be ruthless. It was responsible for killing many people who disagreed with the Soviet system.

Vladimir knew exactly what he wanted, and he held firm. He knew he had to go to a university if he ever wanted to fulfill his dream of working in the KGB. In 1970 Vladimir graduated from high school. He was accepted to Leningrad State University. There he studied international law.

Putin the Spy

Although Putin was anxious that the KGB hadn't contacted him, he waited patiently. He continued his judo practice. He graduated from the university in 1975. Finally, to Putin's relief, the KGB offered him a job. He began studying at the KGB school.

Putin began his career with the KGB working in state security agencies. He met and married Lyudmila. Before long, though, he was sent to East Germany, which had been separated from the rest of Germany after World War II. Some have claimed that Putin might have recruited spies to send to the United States during this time. However, Putin says that he mostly gathered political information in East Germany.

Little information is known about Putin's time in the KGB.

Putin was in the KGB for 16 years, rising to the rank of lieutenant colonel. By then he had grown disillusioned with the KGB and the entire Soviet system.

Vera Dmitrievna Gurevich was one of Putin's grade school teachers. She is often interviewed about her pupil, whom she calls "Volodya":

I thought: this kid will make something of himself. I decided to devote more attention to him and discourage him from hanging around with the boys on the street. He had friends from the neighborhood, two brothers by the name of Kovshov, and he used to prowl around with them, jumping from the roofs of the garages and sheds. Volodya's father didn't like that very much. His papa had very strict morals. But we couldn't get Volodya away from those Kovshov brothers. . . . Volodya himself changed very abruptly in sixth grade. It was obvious; he had set himself a goal. Most likely he had understood that he had to achieve something in life. He began to get better grades, and did it easily.

Source: Vladimir Putin, Nataliya Gevorkyan, Natalya Timakova, and Andrei Kolesnikov. *First Person: An Astonishingly Frank Self-Portrait by Russia's President. New York: PublicAffairs, 2000. Print. Part II.*

What's the Big Idea?

According to Putin's former teacher, a young person can go from a troublemaker to a success. Are you surprised that Putin set such high goals for himself? Do you think people with certain personalities and characteristics are meant to be leaders?

CHAPTER THREE

RISING TO THE PRESIDENCY

s Putin continued rising through the ranks of the KGB, Russia and the Soviet Union were entering a time of turmoil. Many communists felt that Soviet president Mikhail Gorbachev was not following Communist principles. In August 1991, the Soviet military and the Communist Party tried to stage a coup. They attempted to overthrow the government and Gorbachev. The

After leaving the KGB, Putin held various government positions, rising to prime minister and eventually becoming president.

Communism

The former Soviet Union was based on the system of communism. In communism, means of production, such as farms or factories, are supposed to be collectively owned by the people. Usually, farms and factories are actually under government control. Under the ideals of communism, resources such as food are divided among the people according to their needs. However, the results of Russian communism did not work according to the ideal. Many people still lived in poverty. Many in the government became rich and powerful. Communism also restricted a great many rights and freedoms. After the Soviet Union dissolved in 1991, Russia was no longer officially communist.

coup failed. Gorbachev was restored to the presidency, thanks to the efforts of Russian political leader Boris Yeltsin. But Gorbachev no longer had much real power. Yeltsin seemed to be in charge. The conflict had shaken up the entire Soviet Union. One by one, the countries in the Soviet Union began declaring independence. By December 1991, the Soviet Union had collapsed. Yeltsin became president of an independent Russia.

A Political Career

In 1991 Putin resigned from the KGB. He began working as an adviser to Saint Petersburg's mayor. By 1994 he was first deputy mayor of Saint Petersburg. In 1996 Putin moved to Moscow, Russia's capital, to work for President Yeltsin. Shortly afterward, Yeltsin named Putin to several high offices. He seemed to be preparing Putin to be his successor. The president eventually made Putin the head of the FSB. This was the intelligence organization that replaced the KGB.

In August 1999, Yeltsin appointed Putin as his prime minister. No one expected him to last. There had been five prime ministers in the previous 18 months. Yeltsin had fired them all. But Putin would surprise his country. Yeltsin didn't fire him, and the Russian public seemed to like him. Putin's approval ratings were high, even as the president's were dropping. Yeltsin had been accused of corruption throughout his presidency. He faced serious health issues. The Russian people blamed Yeltsin for food

By the late 1990s, Yeltsin had become very unpopular. Russians seemed ready for a change in leadership.

shortages and other issues facing the country. At a time when many Russians viewed Yeltsin as a weak and corrupt leader, Putin was seen as a strong, honest leader.

A Tough President

When Yeltsin resigned in 1999, Putin became acting president. Putin quickly set about campaigning for the next election, only three months away. He won with 53 percent of the vote.

Putin began his term with extremely high popularity. The Russian people saw him as the opposite of Yeltsin. Putin seemed honest and decisive. He was a strong leader who worked to get the people on his side. He made deals with powerful businessmen known as oligarchs to get their support. The Russian economy improved. Relations between Russia and the United States and European countries were

The Oligarchs

An oligarchy is a government that is controlled by a small group of people. In Russia, a group of businesspeople known as the Russian oligarchs became very rich during the 1990s. Some of them also had strong influence in the government. When Putin came to office, he had some conflicts with the wealthy oligarchs. Eventually they struck a bargain. Putin would let them keep their property, including farms and factories established during the Communist years. In exchange, the oligarchs would do everything they could to support Putin. Some of Putin's friends and colleagues made so much money after his rise to power that they also became oligarchs.

relatively good. Russia had faced many challenges in the 1990s. Now the country seemed to be on track to restoring its place as a world power, as it had been when it was part of the Soviet Union. Most Russians believed that Putin was behind all of these positive changes.

However, before long, several incidents hurt Putin's reputation. In August 2000, the Russian submarine *Kursk* sank, killing 118 crew members. Some Russians claimed that the government response was too slow. They thought that the public was lied to about the circumstances surrounding the sinking. People criticized Putin for remaining on vacation during the disaster.

Then, in 2002, a group of more than 50 armed Chechen rebels took 850 civilians hostage in a Moscow theater. The Russian military responded, eventually pumping a poisonous gas into the building. Nearly 130 hostages died as a result of the gas. Other countries, including the United States, criticized

Russian soldiers stand outside the Russian theater where Chechen rebels were holding hundreds of civilians as hostages in October 2002.

Putin's handling of the crisis. However, Putin's ratings inside Russia went higher. He was seen as someone who would do whatever it took to protect Russia against terrorism.

In March 2004, Putin was elected to a second presidential term with 71 percent of the vote. Later that year, another hostage crisis took place at a school. When Russian forces stormed the school, more than 300 hostages, mostly children, were killed.

On May 7, 2004, Putin was inaugurated to his second term as president.

Many details about how the hostages were killed were unknown. People questioned whether the media had been allowed to report the full story.

During his second term as president, Putin took steps to prevent terrorism and increase the president's power. He announced that regional governors would no longer be elected. Instead the president would appoint them.

At the time, Russian presidents were allowed to serve only two consecutive terms. That meant that Putin would be forced to step down in 2008. Just before he left office, he made some changes that gave the prime minister more power. Putin's ally, Dmitri Medvedev, was elected president in 2008. He appointed Putin as prime minister. Many believed that Putin was still really the one in charge.

FURTHER EVIDENCE

This chapter discusses several different events from Putin's presidency, including the 2004 hostage crisis at a Russian school. What was one of the main points about the hostage crisis? The website at the link below also discusses the Beslan school siege. Find a quote from the website. Does the quote support an existing point? Or does it provide a new piece of evidence?

Beslan School Siege
www.mycorelibrary.com/vladimir-putin

CHAPTER FOUR

A REGION
IN CRISIS

Although Medvedev was president from 2008 to 2012, Prime Minister Putin was as powerful as ever. The term was a challenging one for Putin. Along with much of the rest of the world, Russia faced a global economic crisis. Relations were tense between Russia and the United States and many European countries. In 2011 the Russian government was accused of rigging the

Dmitri Medvedev, left, may have been president from 2008 to 2012, but most Russians suspected Putin was still in charge.

elections so that their preferred candidates won seats in parliament. Thousands of Russians protested. They blamed Putin for the fraud. Despite these challenges, Putin ran for president in 2012. He won a third term as president that year, although many accused him of rigging the election so he could win. Many anti-Putin protests followed the election. However, Putin remained in charge.

A Third Term

As his third presidential term began, Putin had been in power for more than 12 years. But he faced new challenges and criticisms. In 2013 Putin's government passed a law widely seen as suppressing the rights of the lesbian, gay, bisexual, and transgendered (LGBT) community. People around the world spoke out against the law. The new law was announced several months before the 2014 Winter Olympic Games in Sochi, Russia. Some people protested by boycotting the games.

Later in 2014, Russia took another action that drew criticism from many world leaders. Russian troops entered the Crimean Peninsula, which was legally a part of the independent nation of Ukraine, and took it over. Putin has argued that the people in Crimea are mostly of Russian background. When the Soviet Union collapsed, he thought the Crimean Peninsula should have been made part of Russia.

On March 16, 2014, the people of Crimea held a vote, and 95 percent of

Sochi Winter Olympics

During the Winter Olympics, people from many countries compete against each other in such sports as skiing, figure skating, speed skating, and bobsledding. The 2014 Winter Olympics were held in Sochi, Russia, a city on the Black Sea. This resort city with a mild climate is located near the Caucasus Mountains. The Sochi games were the most expensive in history, costing about $51 billion. Much of that money went toward building things that were needed to accommodate so many visitors. New roads, power plants, arenas, stadiums, and hotels were constructed for the games.

Protestors in London, England, hold signs criticizing Putin and Russia's policies that discriminate against gay people.

them voted to leave Ukraine and join Russia. Many believed that Putin's government had rigged the vote in Russia's favor. But Crimea once again became part of Russia.

Unrest and conflict continued in Ukraine. Pro-Russian demonstrators, who support Crimea becoming part of Russia, took over buildings. Clashes led to street battles, gunfire, and arson. Some of the protesters were Ukrainian. But many people believed that Russia had sent Russian troops into Ukraine disguised as pro-Russian demonstrators. Concerned about the violence in the region, other countries responded. The United States set trade limits aimed at Russian businesses, hoping to

The Crimean Peninsula

People have been fighting over the Crimean Peninsula since ancient Roman times. This is largely because it has ports in the Black Sea, including a valuable naval base. The Crimean Peninsula is a body of land that juts out from Ukraine into the Black Sea. Crimea became part of the Soviet Union in 1954. When the Soviet Union broke up in 1991, Crimea became part of Ukraine. In 2014 a combination of Russian armed intervention and an internal vote returned Crimea to Russia. Today Crimea's economy depends mostly on tourism and natural gas.

The world will continue watching Putin's actions in Crimea and elsewhere.

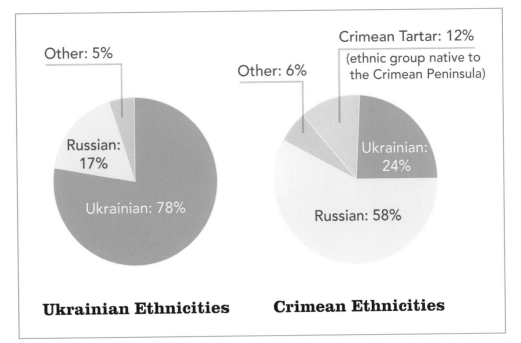

Ukrainian Ethnicities

Other: 5%

Russian: 17%

Ukrainian: 78%

Crimean Ethnicities

Other: 6%

Crimean Tartar: 12% (ethnic group native to the Crimean Peninsula)

Ukrainian: 24%

Russian: 58%

Ukrainian and Crimean Populations

Look at the population breakdown for all of the country of Ukraine. Now look at the population of Crimea. Does this information support Crimea becoming part of Russia? What else can you learn about Ukraine and Crimea from these numbers?

pressure Putin into ending the conflict. But fighting continued through the summer of 2014.

Headline Maker

Vladimir Putin remains a controversial figure. Some think he is a dictator who has achieved power through less-than-fair means. Many others inside Russia see

Putin and other Russian authorities watch the 2014 Winter Olympics closing ceremonies in Sochi.

Putin as a strong leader who is restoring Russia's power and influence in the world. Regardless of the world's opinions about his actions, President Putin is one of today's top newsmakers.

On March 18, 2014, Putin gave a speech in which he discussed his belief that Crimea should belong to Russia:

> Now, many years later, I heard residents of Crimea say that back in 1991 they were handed over like a sack of potatoes. This is hard to disagree with. And what about the Russian state? . . . The country was going through such hard times then that realistically it was incapable of protecting its interests. However, the people could not reconcile themselves to this outrageous historical injustice. All these years, citizens and many public figures came back to this issue, saying that Crimea is historically Russian. . . . Yes, we all knew this in our hearts and minds, but we had to proceed from the existing reality and build out good-neighborly relations with independent Ukraine on a new basis. Meanwhile, our relations with Ukraine, with the fraternal Ukrainian people, have always been and will remain of foremost importance for us.
>
> Source: The Kremlin, Moscow. "Full Text of Putin's Speech on Crimea." Prague Post. Prague Post, March 18, 2014. Web. Accessed August 8, 2014.

Changing Minds

People can decide that land belongs to a country in several ways. Decide whether you think Crimea should belong to Russia or Ukraine. Then write a short essay trying to convince someone of your opinion.

IMPORTANT DATES

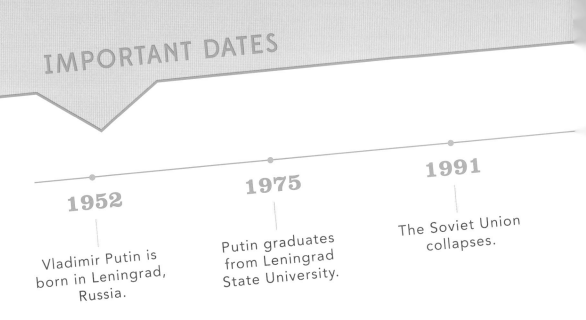

1952

Vladimir Putin is born in Leningrad, Russia.

1975

Putin graduates from Leningrad State University.

1991

The Soviet Union collapses.

2002

The Moscow theater hostage crisis leads to the deaths of approximately 130 hostages.

2004

Putin is elected to his second term as Russian president.

2004

More than 330 people, many of them students, are killed in the Beslan School hostage crisis.

1994

Putin becomes deputy mayor of Saint Petersburg.

1999

Putin becomes acting president of Russia.

2000

Putin is elected president of Russia for his first term.

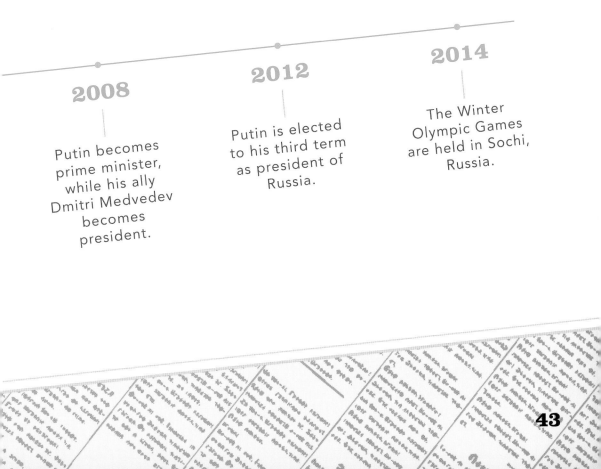

2008

Putin becomes prime minister, while his ally Dmitri Medvedev becomes president.

2012

Putin is elected to his third term as president of Russia.

2014

The Winter Olympic Games are held in Sochi, Russia.

STOP AND THINK

Take a Stand

In this book, you learned that Crimea went from being part of Ukraine to being part of Russia. Think about other countries and regions that used to be part of the Soviet Union. Do you think they should return to being part of Russia? Why or why not?

Say What?

When you learn about politics, history, and foreign countries, there are a lot of new words to learn. Find five words in this book that you've never heard or read before. Look them up, and then write definitions for them in your own words.

Tell the Tale

Imagine that you are Putin when he was a badly behaved boy who got into fights. Write 200 words about the moment when you decided to turn your life around. What changed your outlook? What parts of your old ways will you keep, and which will you put aside forever?

Surprise Me

Chapter Five talks about current events involving Putin. Some of his decisions have surprised world leaders. What do you find most surprising about Putin's recent actions? Pick two or three things that surprise you, and write a few sentences about them.

GLOSSARY

ally
a person or country that supports or helps another person or country

arson
the criminal act of deliberately setting fires

boycott
to refuse to work with, purchase from, or visit an organization or country as a form of protest

corruption
illegal or dishonest behavior, especially by someone in power

coup
a sudden takeover of the government, often with violence

disillusioned
having lost trust or faith in something

hostage
a person who is captured and held until certain demands have been met

parliament
a group of people elected to make laws

ruthless
cruel, merciless, without remorse

terrorist
one who uses threats or violence to get what they want

LEARN MORE

Books

Murray, Julie. *Russia*. Minneapolis: ABDO, 2014.

Murray, Julie. *Ukraine*. Minneapolis: ABDO, 2014.

Websites

To learn more about Newsmakers, visit **booklinks.abdopublishing.com**. These links are routinely monitored and updated to provide the most current information available.

Visit **www.mycorelibrary.com** for free additional tools for teachers and students.

INDEX

ABOUT THE AUTHOR

Lu Sylvan is the author of many books for children, including the Animal Bites series of wildlife books. She lives with her family on the Florida coast.